Knitting Patterns

for the

Hand Spinner

Knitting Patterns

for the

Hand Spinner

Knitting Patterns

for the

Hand Spinner

This is the second in the series of knitting patterns, designed by Claire Boley for the hand spinner.

1st booklet – Scarves and Waistcoats.

2nd booklet – Hats, Mittins and Gloves.

3rd booklet – Jumpers and Slipovers.

Introduction

As a young girl I would sit spellbound watching my grandmother knitting for the family. As I was so fascinated grandmother suggested she should teach me. Using commercial wool I knitted scarves for my teddy bears and dolls. By the time I was 13 years old I was knitting jumpers for myself following commercial knitting patterns.

In my late 20's I was taught to spin different fibres at an evening class. A few years later I was lucky enough to be introduced to Ann Lander by a friend. Ann taught me to spin flax.

I have enjoyed hand knitting and hand spinning for many years and have been privileged to be a full member of The Somerset Guild of Craftsmen, designing my own knitwear, holding workshops and solo exhibitions across the South West of England.

Acknowledgment

Thank you Anna Robinson for being the model for the garments.

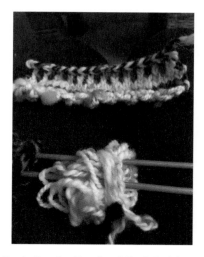

A practice knit, using Texel and Black Welsh Mountain fleece, with natural dyes.

This is the 2nd Booklet in the series of Knitting Patterns for the Hand Spinner, designed by Claire Boley.

Hats, Mittins and Gloves.

Contents

Naturally Dyed wool that you could use for your Beani

A beani - for when it's cold

Pattern – 3 sizes, using hand spun, worsted type, double knitting yarn, from a black welsh mountain fleece. While plying your singles you could always add small amounts of coloured yarn, to make it into a Slub yarn (page 42) to use for the first 3 rows of your beani.

Using size 3 1/4 (10) needles, cast on 104, (108,112) sts and work the first 3 rows in st st.

With the right side facing start the double rib.

1st K1 P2 *K2 P2 rep. from*to the last st k1

2nd row P1 K2 *P2 k2 rep. from* to the last st P1

Rep. these 2 rows for 9cm (3 1/2inches)

Change to size 4mm (8) needles. Rep. the 2 rows as above for 18cm (7inches) from the beginning, ending with the 2nd row.

8

Shape the crown.

1st row K1 P2tog * k2 p2tog rep. from * to the last stitch k1. 78, (81, 84sts)

2nd row p1 k1 * p2 k1 rep from * to last st p1.

3rd row k1 * p1 k2 rep. from * to last 2 sts p1 k1.

4th row as 2nd row.

5th row k1 p1 * K2 tog. p1 rep. from * to the last stitch k1. 53 (55, 57) sts.

6th row p1 * k1 rep. from * to end

7th row k1 * p1 k1 rep. from * to end

8th row as 6th row.

9th row k1* k2tog. rep. from * to end 27(28,29) sts.

10th row P1* p2tog. Rep. from * to last stitch P1. 14 (15, 15) sts.

Break the yarn, making sure it is long enough to thread through the remaining stitches and to sew up the seam using an invisible stitch.

How to make a pompom for your Beani

Cut 2 pieces of card into 8cm (3 inch) circles, then 2
smaller circles in the centre of both pieces of card,
these should be 3cm (1 ¼ inches)

Measuring the card

Winding the yarn

Once the two cards are cut put them together and
start winding the yarn around the ring until the hole

is completely full. Now work around the outside edge with a pair of sharp scissors cutting through all the layers of yarn, once this is done take a long length of yarn tie it around the middle of the pompom as tightly as possible, after doing this pull the cards away from the pompom. You are now left with a pompom which may need to be trimmed before fixing it tightly to the Beani.

Beret

Pattern - 3 sizes.

Using size 3 1/4 (10) needles cast on 84, (94,108 sts) work 9 rows in k1 p1 rib.

Next row Rib 1 * m 1, rib 2, rep from * to last st, m1 rib 1 126, (141,162} sts

Next row k.

Next row p3, (7, 9)* m1 p7 (7,11 rep from * to last 4, (8, 10) sts m1 p4 (8, 10) 144, (160,176) sts

Change to no 4mm (8 needles) and starting with a knit row work 14, (18,20) rows in st st.

Shape the beret as follows -

1st row k 1 * k2 tog, k16 (18, 20) rep from * to the last 17(19, 21) sts k2 tog k to the end 136 (152, 168) sts.

2nd and every alternant row p.

3rd row k1 * k2tog k15, (17, 19) rep from * to the last 16 (18, 20) sts k2 tog k to the end 128(144,160) sts.

5th row K1 * k2 tog, k14 (16, 18) rep from * to last 15 (17,19) sts k2 tog k to the end 120 (136,152) sts.

7th row k1 * k2tog k13 (15,17) sts rep from * to last 14 (16, 18) sts k2 tog, k to the end 112 (128, 144) sts
9th row k1 * k2 tog k12 (14,16) rep from * to last 13 (15, 17) sts k2 tog 104 (120,136) sts.

Continue decreasing in this way working one stitch less between each decrease st until 24 sts remain – ending with a decrease row. Next row p1,* p2 tog rep from * to the last st, p1 (13 sts).

Break off a length of yarn, long enough to thread through the remaining sts and for sewing up the seam with an invisible stitch.

Bobbles or Pompom which is it going to be?

 Now is the time to decide whether to make a pompom (page 10) or a couple of bobbles (page 26) to go in the centre at the top of the beret.

If you don't fancy either in the centre of the beret, why not put a loop of a 12 crocheted chain on the top in a colour that's different from your beret. You could always put a bobble then add the loop through the middle of the bobble – both in different colours.

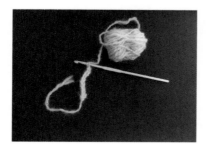

Making 12 crocheted chains for the loop.

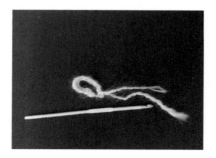

The chains made into a loop.

Beret made from a Jacob Fleece

Knit this Jacob's fleece beret using **the pattern on page 12**, 4 rows cream, 4 rows brown, in **knob yarn.**

*Using the brown part of the fleece, fill 2 bobbins with worsted type, Z singles. Ply these 2 yarns together S twist. While plying decorate the core yarn, with knobs - for the knob yarn. (It's the spinner's own choice which yarn is used as the core yarn)

Make the knob yarn by going backwards and forwards for 1.25 cm (1/2 inch) 3 or 4 times at intervals of 7cm (3 inches)

*Repeat the knob yarn when plying the cream part of the fleece.

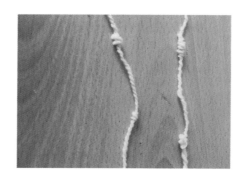

Knob Yarn

Jacob sheep

A beret made from silk and wool

The main part of this beret was spun 50/50 with Mulberry silk along with Texel fleece which was dyed from Brazil exhaust.

*First fill 2 bobbins with 4 ply worsted type yarn. 1 with Texel fleece (without dye) the other with Mulberry silk, ply these together. This yarn is to be used for the 3 rows st st **and the remainder of the rib.

Now fill 2 bobbins with a worsted type Z singles (1 Texel dyed, 2 Mulberry silk) S Ply them together making a worsted type 4 ply yarn, to be used for the blanket st row and the main part of the beret.

Pattern is on Page 12

Cast on with * then work the** first 3 rows in stocking stitch

4th row work in blanket stitch (page19) using the mulberry silk with dyed Texel fleece.

Next row finish the rib for the pattern on page 12 using wool without dye / silk.

Change over to the main colour (texel with dye and silk} for the main part of the beret.

Edgings

Here are 2 Fancy edgings I sometimes use for my berets and mittins.

Rolled Edging

Cast on the sts in main colour st st 2 rows.

st st 2 more rows - this time in the 2nd colour.

5th row *With the front facing and still using the (2nd colour) knit 5 stitches – take the right hand needle with sts and roll it over backwards until the knitting is back facing the front again, repeat this from * to the end of the row.

Tip If you would like a wider rolled edge, increase the number of rows making sure that the front of your work is facing you before you make the roll. Once the roll is made I recommend that you knit an extra couple of rows in single rib before starting the main part of the beret.

Beret with the rolled edge

Blanket stitch edging

Cast on with the main colour – stocking stitch – 3 rows.

4th row (front facing) using a different colour yarn, single rib 4 stitches * take the yarn around the knitting and up to the front ready to do the next stitch rib 4 repeat from *to the end of the row.

Making a blanket stitch

Taking the yarn under and around the back of the stitches,

.

More naturally dyed yarn

knitted Hats

4 knitted hats, using the same pattern but different fleece and colour.

1st hat is made from Blue faced Leicester fleece with natural dyes

2nd is from a Wensleydale fleece with 2 shades of Alpaca fibre.

3rd is from a Blue Faced Leicester Fleece - white and grey.

4th is from a Black Welsh Mountain fleece with Natural Dyes.

The first 3 hats have been spun from fleece with a staple length of 10cm (4 inches) or more and spun into a worsted type yarn.

The forth hat has been spun from a rolag using the long draw technique (woollen yarn) with a short staple fleece, which was less than 10cm (4 inches) in length.

A woollen yarn can be spun into any thickness, from fine to very thick by the spinner adjusting their own technique as well as adjusting the tension adjustment screw. This yarn is warmer than a worsted type yarn due to the air being trapped between the fibres while carding. It will be noticed that the carded fibres go around and around when spun from a rolag, instead of in a parallel line as they do when being spun into a worsted type yarn from a combed lock or roving.

The worsted type yarn can be spun straight from a fleece which is in very good condition, such as one that has been shorn in the last few days. If the locks are matted open them up by teasing and drawing out the fibres from both ends by using either your fingers or a dog comb. These fibres should be aligned in the direction of the yarn when being spun with the tips of the locks facing the orifice, and spun using the short drafting action.

Combing a lock with a dog comb

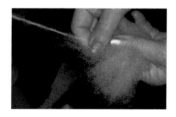

Spinning from a folded lock.

Pattern - 1 size

Brim

Using size 4mm (8) needles cast on 35 sts Work 47cm (19 inches) in single moss st. Cast off.

Main part

Using size 4mm (8) needles cast on 128 sts

Work in double rib for 13cm (5 inches)

1st row slip 1 k2 p2 to last st k1

2nd row slip 1 p2 k2 to last st k1

Shape the crown

1st row slip1 k2 * p2 tog k2 from * to last 3 sts k3

2nd row slip1 * p2 tog k1 from * to end

3rd row slip1 k2 tog 32 times (33 sts)

4th row slip 1 p2 tog 15 times k2tog 17sts.

Break a length of yarn, long enough to sew up the seams and to thread through the remaining stitches. Turn the brim and the crown inside out. Using an invisible stitch, join the brim to the crown before joining up the side seam.

Rolled Brimed Hats

Hats 1 and 2

3rd hat

1st hat. Black Welsh Mountain fleece has been used. The naturally dyed fleece was added while carding.

2nd hat. The main colour is brown from a Shetland fleece, with naturally dyed fleece added while carding to make rolags for a woollen yarn. A small

25

amount of mohair fibre was added over the top while plying.

3rd hat. This was made from a Jacob's fleece which has been separated out into the 2 colours dark brown and cream. It is up to the spinner whether the yarn is spun woollen or semi worsted. On the top of this particular hat is a bobble knitted from the dark brown wool.

Bobble. Using 3 1/4mm (9) needles cast on 3 stitches and working in stocking stitch increase 1 stitch each end of every k row until you have 7 stitches. Decrease 1 stitch each end of the k row until 3 stitches remain. Cast off the remaining 3 stitches, leaving at least 15 cm (6 inches) of thread to tidy up the bobble and sew it onto the top of the hat once the seams have been sewn up.

Pattern - 2 sizes

Cast on 104 (108) sts using size 4mm (8) needles.

Starting with K st, work in st st for 23cm (9 inches) 24cm (9 1/2 inches)

Ending with the P row.

To shape the crown and still working in st st.

1st row, with the front facing.* K2 tog k 22 (23) k2 tbl repeat from * to end.

2nd and every alternate row P.

3rd row, * k2 tog k20 (21) k2 tog tbl rep from * to end.

5th row, * k2 tog k18 (19) k2tog tbl repeat from * to the end.

Continue working 2 stitches less between dec. on every alternate row until 16 (20) stitches remain, ending with the right side facing for the next row.

Next row (**2nd size only**) k2 tog k6 k2 tog tbl twice – 16 sts.

Next row P.

Next (both sizes) *k2 tog, k2 tog tbl. rep from* to the end – 8 sts

Break a length of the yarn long enough to thread through the remaining stitches and to sew up the seams. First draw up the stitches tightly and fasten off securely. With the hat the right way round, using an invisible stitch join the back seam for the rolled brim -(17cm (6 1/2inches). Now turn the hat inside out and use the same stitch for the crown.

A square shaped hat with a rolled brim

The brim of this hat has been knitted using a Blue Faced Leicester fleece, which had been spun into a worsted type yarn.

The main part has also been spun into a worsted type yarn - 1 bobbin has a Blue Faced Leicester fleece, the 2nd bobbin has naturally dyed fleece, plyed together to make a 4 ply yarn.

The buttons were made from oven baked clay and were painted with acrylic paint with varnish painted over the top. (Do not wash the hat with the buttons in position)

Pattern 1 size

* Brim - Cast on 90 stitches using 3 3/4mm (9) needles

Work in single moss stitch for 7cm (3 inches)

Change to size 4mm (8 needles) continue to work straight in moss stitch for 12 inches from*

Now cast off. Leaving a length of yarn long enough for sewing up the seams with an invisible stitch. Once the hat is sewn up turn it the right way around with the front facing. Take the 2 pointed corners at the top of the hat and fold them over towards the centre - sew in position, now add the buttons or if you prefer make 2 plaits out of the spun yarn and sew them on each corner then tie them together in the centre.

The top of a square hat tied in a bow with a woollen plait.

Round Hats

Hat 1

Hat 2

Both of these hats have been knitted from the same pattern, in garter stitch, with a woollen plaited bow for the top.

Hat 1 has been spun from Texel fleece/Mulberry silk 50/50. Slub yarn has been used for the first 4 rows using a naturally dyed wool.

Hat 2, has been knitted using different shades of fleece, the main colour being cream from a Texel fleece. The pink is the exhaust from the natural dye - Brazil wood.

Pattern - 1 size

Using size 3 1/4mm (10 needles) cast on 94 sts working in garter stitch for 8 cm (3 inches).

Change to size 4mm (8) needles.

 1st row inc. 1st every 4th st. to the end of row – 117sts.

Work in garter st. for 18cm (7 inches)

Shape the crown.

1st row K1 * K2tog K5 repeat from * to end.

2nd row and with every alternate row, garter st. with out a dec.

3rd row K1 * K2tog k5 repeat from * to end

5th row K1 * k2tog k4 repeat from * to end.

 Continue to dec this way until 31 stitches remain. Last row K1 * K2tog repeat from * to end. Take a length of yarn long enough to thread through the remaining stitches and to sew up the seam using an invisible stitch.

Fingerless Mittins

This is the pattern for all 3 pairs of mittins

If you find you need larger mittins use larger size needles and add a few more rows to the thumb gusset, without adding more stitches.

When you have finished knitting each finger and thumb make sure that you break off a length of the yarn long enough for sewing up the seams.

Right hand

Use size 3 1/4mm (10) needles for the cuffs and 33/4mm (9) needles for the main part with 4 ply yarn.

If you find you are using too thick a wool ie double knitting, use size 3 3/4mm (9) needles for the cuff and size 4mm (8) needles for the main part.

Cast on 38sts, work in single rib 10cm (4 inches) or longer if you wish.

Increase 1 st each end of the last row 40 sts

Change to size 3 3/4mm (9) needles

With the front facing work in stocking stitch, work the thumb gusset as follows -

1st row K 20 sts P1 K2 P! K to the end.

2nd row K1 P15 K1 P2 K1 P to last st K1

3rd row K20 P1 m1 k2 m1 P1 k to the end.

4th row k1 P15 K1 P4 k1 P to the last st k1.

5th row K20 P 1 K4 P1 k to end.

6th row as 4th row.

7th row K20 P1 m1 k4 m1 P1 k to the end.

Continue like this inc 1st at each side of the thumb gusset on every 4th row until there are 12 sts between the 2p sts. (50 sts)

Work 1 row.

Work thumb.

1st row k20 p1 k12 turn

2nd row k1 p11 cast on 2 turn.

Work 3 rows st st.

Work 2 rows in single rib. Cast off.

With the right side facing pick up 2 sts from the 2 cast on sts at the base of the thumb. K to the end (40sts)

Work a k st at both ends of every row.

Work 7 rows in st st.

1st finger with the right side facing

1st row k 26 turn.

2nd row k1 p 11 k1 cast on 2 sts, turn.

Work 3 rows st st.

Work 2 rows single rib.

Cast off.

Second finger

With the right side facing, rejoin the yarn and knit up 2 sts from the 2 cast on sts at the base of the 1st finger. k5 turn.

Next row –K1 P11 cast on 2sts turn. K1 stitch at each end of every row.

*Work 3 rows in st st,

 2 rows in single rib.

 Cast off.

Third finger

With the right side facing rejoin the yarn and knit up 2 stitches from the 2 cast-on sts at the base of the second finger k5 turn.

Next row- k1 P11 cast on 2 sts turn *finish this finger as 2nd finger

Forth finger

With the right side facing, rejoin the yarn and

knit up 2 sts from the cast on stitches at the base of the 3rd finger k4 turn.

Next row K1 p8 k1 turn. K1 st at each end of every row.

Work 3 rows in st st

2 rows in single rib. Cast off

Left hand

Using size 3 1/4mm (10) needles cast on 38 sts work in single rib for (10cm-4inches) inc. 1 stitch each end of the last row – 40 sts.

Change to size3 3/4mm (9) needles

Work in stocking stitch for thumb gusset as follows-

1st row K16 p1 k2 p1 k to the end.

2nd row k1 p19 k1 p2 k1 p to the last st k1

3rd row k16 p1 m1 k2 m1 p1 k to the end.

4th row k1 p19 k1 p4 k1 p to the last st k1.

5th row k16 p1 k4 p1 k to the end.

6th row as 4th row.

7th row K16 P1 m1 K4 m1 p1 k to end.

Continue like this increasing 1st at each end of the thumb gusset on every 4th row until there are 12 sts between the P2 sts.

Work 1 row

Work thumb as follows (front facing).

1st row k16 P1 K12 cast on 2 sts turn

2nd row k1 P12 K1 turn.

Work 3 rows in st st,

2 rows in single rib.

Cast off.

With the right side facing knit up 2sts from the 2 cast on sts at the base of the thumb K to end 40 sts.

Work one K st at both ends of every row, work 7 rows in stocking stitch.

First finger

1st row K26 cast on 2 turn.

2nd row K1 P12 k1 turn.

Work 3 rows st st.

Single rib 2 rows. Cast off.

Second finger

With the right side facing, rejoin yarn and k up 2 sts from the 2 cast on sts at the base of the first finger K5 cast on 2 sts turn.

 Next row K1 P12 K1 turn.

Work 3 rows st st.

Single rib 2 rows.

Cast off.

Third finger

With the right side facing, rejoin the yarn and k up 2 sts from the base of the second finger k5 cast on 2 turn.

Next row k1 p12 k1 turn.

Work 3 rows in stocking stitch,

2 rows in single rib.

Cast off.

Forth finger

With the right side facing, rejoin the yarn and knit up 2 sts from 2 cast on sts at the base of the third finger k 4 turn.

Next row k1 p8 k1.

Work 3 rows in st st.

2 rows in single rib.

Cast off. Sew up the mittins using an invisible seam.

Gloves

Knit the basic pattern as shown above but instead of knitting 3 rows stocking stitch and 2 rows in single rib for the thumb and fingers, work as below, making sure you leave a long enough length of yarn for sewing up the seams of the fingers and thumbs.

Thumb 14 rows, stocking stitch.

Shape top – 1 row K2 tog 7 times.

2nd row k1 p to last st k1.

3rd row k2 tog 3 times k1. Break off yarn.

Thread through remaining sts. Draw up and fasten off securely.

1st finger 16 rows. Shape top as thumb.

2nd finger 18 rows. Shape top as thumb.

3rd finger 16 rows. Shape top as thumb.

4th finger 12 rows. Shape top - 1st row k2 tog 5 times.

 2nd row k1 p to last st k1.

3rd row k2 tog twice k1.

 Tip Knit a few more or less rows before shaping the fingers if they are short or too long for the number of rows mentioned for the gloves.

Any of these designs can be used for a pair of gloves.

Naturally Dyed Wool

Design for the 1st pair of fingerless mittins

How to knit the design for these mittins.

(The main pattern for these starts on page 32)

Cast on in the shade of grey - Jacob cross – worsted type yarn.

Working in single rib. With the front facing work the 1st row in red (Dye - Madder) next row yellow (Dye - Onion skins) Continue in single rib for the cuff 8cm (4 inches) using the grey wool.

If you would like longer cuffs work a few more rows, making sure that both cuffs are the same length. Still working in single rib and using the grey yarn, increase 1st at the beginning and end of the next row – 40sts

Next row *rib 4 make a bobble in between 4th and 5th st. rib 4 make another bobble in between the next 4th and 5th st. repeat from * to the end of the row alternating the colour of the bobbles as you knit.

How to make the bobbles for these mittins

Pick up 3 sts between the 4th and 5th st with the red or yellow yarn. Turn -

P1 row.

K1 row increase I st at each end of this row (5sts)

P1 row.

K1 row increase 1 st at each end (7sts)

P1 row.

K1 row k 2 sts tog at each end of this row (5sts)

P1 row.

K1 row k2 tog at each end (3st)

Next row, cast off the 3 stitches, tie the ends of the yarn for the knitted bobble tightly together then sew the bobble in position. With the front facing k4 sts before starting the next bobble.

The cuffs along with the thumbs and fingers for these mittins are knitted in stocking stitch using the grey wool.

Palms are knitted in stocking stitch using the cream colour.

When spinning the yarn for the backs of the mittins fill 1 bobbin with Z cream, 2nd bobbin with Z grey, S ply together while adding the natural dyes over the top (slub yarn) then knit in single moss stitch.

Slub Yarn. Fill 2 bobbins of single Z twist yarn. S ply them together adding a different colour over the top at 5cm(2inch) intervals, do this by holding small amounts of the coloured yarn in the right hand when treadling very slowly, while S plying.

Slub yarn

2nd pair of fingerless mittins

(The main pattern starts on page 32)

Cuffs, cast on with the naturally dyed plyed wool. Work 2 rows in single rib using the naturally dyed wool.

Next row single rib using the Black wool. Blanket stitch – see page 19. Continue in single rib, for 10cm (4 inches) or longer if you wish =

3 rows black - Black Welsh Mountain fleece.

*2 rows grey - (Masham fleece)

4 rows black.

2 rows grey.

The palms, thumb and fingers are worked in grey. The backs are knitted in single moss stitch 2 rows grey, 2 rows black finishing with 2 rows grey.

The 3rd pair of fingerless mittins

(The main pattern is on page 32)

Cast on the stitches with dyed wool, yellow – onion skins.

St st 3 rows with the dyed wool.

Next row use the fawn yarn in single rib, making a rolled edge - see page 18

2 rows single rib – Black Welsh Mountain fleece

Change to fawn, single rib 2 rows – Shetland fleece

Change to black welsh, single rib 10cm (4inches) – if you would like longer cuffs work a few more rows, making sure each cuff is the same length.

Finish the cuffs with 2 rows in st st - fawn.

Palms, thumbs and fingers are all knitted in black.

Backs of these mittins are knitted in single moss stitch -

4 rows black.

2 rows fawn,

4 rows black.

2 rows fawn.

4 rows black.

Finishing with 2 rows fawn before starting the thumbs, fingers and palms in black.

Buttons and button holes for the cuffs

Do not sew the cuffs together if you are thinking of putting buttons plus button holes along the sides of the cuffs. Get a crochet hook plus the yarn and crochet up and down the sides of the cuffs, making sure you make 2 to 3 button holes along one of the sides. Another button hole can be crocheted on the opposite side for a larger button – this is to hold the mittins together when they're not being worn.

Abreviations

cm – centimetre

dec – decrease

inc – increase

K - knit

m – make

mm – millimetres

p - purl

rep – repeat

st – stitch

sts - stitches

st st – stocking stitch

tbl – through back of loop

tog – together

The End

Claire can be found on Facebook, Twitter, Goodreads and Instagram.

Also by Claire Boley

Hand Spinning with Claire Boley

1. Sheep, Fleece and Carding

2. Spindles and Spinning Wheels

3. Spinning Techniques and different types of fancy yarns

4. Getting hand spun yarn ready for hand knitting

Natural Dyeing for Wool Spinners

Printed in Great Britain
by Amazon